Marketing for the Modern Mindset: A Definitive Guide to Church Marketing

I0528487

By

Lawrence N. Overbey, Jr.

Dedication

I dedicate this book...

To my wife, Yolanda, who stood by my side during the writing, revising, and rewriting of this book. To you, I express my sincere love and thanks.

To my adult children, Lawrence, Kendra, and Emmanuel, I hope my writing of this book inspires you to do incredible things and have an even more positive impact on society.

To my mom and dad, Shirley and Lawrence, thank you for your encouraging words and patience with me during this journey.

About the Author

Lawrence Overbey, a native of Baltimore, Maryland, served in the United States Air Force for 11 years and is an IT Director for a large hospitality company. He is a member of the Board of Directors for Promise686 and a volunteer for the Production Team at Victory Church in Norcross, GA. Lawrence has two older brothers and one older sister. He has been married to Yolanda for over 30 years and has three adult children. Currently living in the Atlanta metro area, Lawrence loves music, plays the piano, and enjoys traveling. He has an MBA from Belhaven University, is the founder of Relevance Ministry Marketing, LLC., and believes that the principles of marketing can aid the local church in reaching their community.

Preface

Throughout my years of leading church community outreach efforts, I was convinced of their effectiveness, yet I always felt something was missing. As I studied Marketing at Belhaven University, the missing piece became clear to me. I realized that I lacked a comprehensive understanding of marketing principles. The more I explored marketing, the more convinced I became that these principles could benefit the church. As a result, I decided to write this book. The writing process was filled with many obstacles and took several years to complete, but I persisted because I remained confident that marketing could enhance the church's outreach efforts.

Interestingly, in 2022, corporations allocated over $480 billion to market their products and services, as stated by Statista. The reason for such a large investment in marketing is that it generates tangible results. The typical return on investment for a successful marketing campaign is estimated to be 400%, with some campaigns yielding even higher returns of 900%. With these numbers in mind, it is possible for the church to experience similar positive outcomes by implementing effective marketing strategies.

I pray that the marketing information presented in this book will contribute to the realization of God's vision for your church while leading to a positive impact on your community for the glory of God.

CONTENTS

Page Left Blank Intentionally

Chapter 1

Introduction

Sharing the gospel of Jesus Christ is an important aspect of our faith; "Go into all the world and preach the gospel to all creation (Mark 16:15)!" The "Good News" of the gospel is that salvation through Jesus Christ is available to everyone, regardless of their background. This good news should be proclaimed all over the world! It is my belief that marketing can play a significant role in the spreading of the "Good News" in ways that are relevant, authentic, and resounding.

It has been my privilege to work with various churches over the years to spread the gospel of Jesus Christ. I have led and assisted with evangelistic training, led teams in door-to-door witnessing, hosted and participated in community outreach conferences, and used many other methods of reaching communities for Christ. I've worked with the North American Mission Board and hosted seasonal outreach efforts like *"The Pumpkin Patch Parable"* and *"Reverse Trick or Treat,"* which were powerful outreach efforts that helped to introduce the church, its mission, and its Master to the community.

I also helped to lead church efforts to implement programs like *"God Rewards Our Work" (G.R.O.W.),* which is an effective church-wide outreach and visitation program for prompting church members to engage in reaching the lost and unchurched in the community for Christ. From the technology side, I have served as a webmaster and designed and developed church websites and utilized social media sites like Facebook, Instagram, and X, formerly named Twitter, to promote the church and help further the message of Christ to the community. Lastly, I helped organize and execute mail campaigns and hosted a seminar on real estate and finance to offer vital information to the local community during the financial housing crisis.

Although some of my outreach initiatives showed modest success, I always felt something was missing. It was during my MBA program at Belhaven University that I discovered how the power of marketing management could enhance churches' outreach efforts. Looking back, I can see how some outreach initiatives were less effective due to a lack of knowledge of the target demographic as well as a failure to craft the right message for the population.

Most assuredly, without understanding the target market, community outreach efforts may yield little or no results and have no visible impact on the church or on the Kingdom of God.

By emphasizing the importance of understanding and connecting with one's audience, this book provides valuable insights that can be adapted to a variety of contexts. To this end, I have included a variety of integral marketing elements, such as the 5 Ps of marketing, social media advertising, organizational growth cycles, and the concept of segmenting, targeting, and positioning (STP), which are all fundamental to the accomplishment of any fruitful marketing plan.

While this book primarily focuses on strategies for promoting and growing the church community, the principles and tactics presented can certainly be applied to other businesses and organizations as well. Whether you're pastoring a local church or running a small business, this book offers practical advice and actionable tips for building a strong brand, engaging with customers or supporters, and achieving long-term success.

There is no doubt that marketing has revolutionized the way secular organizations reach their audience, and churches should be no exception. I believe that the principles of marketing, if properly applied, can help church leaders better understand and meet the needs of their community. In a world where people spend most of their time online, churches can use digital marketing strategies to connect with people far and wide to share the gospel. With social media platforms like Facebook, YouTube, Instagram, and X, formerly named Twitter, churches can easily create and share content that engages their audience, drives traffic to their website, and ultimately get people to walk through the church doors.

As a member of Victory Church in Norcross,

Georgia, I have observed how Victory has deployed various biblical and marketing principles to reach their local community, positively impact the world at large, and build a healthy church.

Under the direction of Senior Pastor Johnson and Summer Bowie and under the careful guidance of Founding Pastors Dennis and Colleen Rouse, Victory has become a multi-cultural, multi-ethnic model for other churches to aspire to. My first interaction with Victory Church was in 1998, when I arrived in Georgia after 11 years of service in the United States Air Force.

Since that time, Victory has grown from a church in a single building to amassing four physical campuses and one online campus and recently launched 50 house churches, bringing the church to those in the community who may never grace the doors of the local church. Prayerfully, after implementing the marketing principles and information offered in this book, your church will realize its vision and continue to effectively reach the community for the Kingdom of God.

Chapter 2

Marketing Misconceptions

Some church leaders have misconceptions about marketing. I know because I was once one of those church leaders. I recall being invited to a marketing seminar while serving as the Director of Community Outreach for a Baptist Church in Norcross, GA. During that time, I remember stating that marketing had no place in the church, and as a result, I refused to attend the session. In the years following, other church leaders invited me to similar marketing seminars, but my disdain for church marketing remained intact. After completing a course in marketing while pursuing an MBA with **Belhaven University**, I began to rethink my position on marketing and began to see how marketing could be an effective tool for reaching communities for Christ.

Shortly after completing my studies, I offered to write a marketing plan for a church where I served as a worship leader. After seeing the marketing plan, the staff pastor quickly told me that I could not use the word marketing in the church. He also stated that the term marketing would be rejected by the congregation, not to mention that "marketing" was a secular term.

It is apparent that different people define marketing differently. Unfortunately, many of the definitions used to define marketing are based on assumptions or past experiences and not based on the proper usage or meaning of the term.

A basic definition for marketing, and one that I will use extensively in this book, is "marketing is identifying and meeting human and social needs," I believe this concept of identifying needs and fulfilling them is absolutely supported in the scripture. God sent Jesus into the world to save the world from their sins (John 3:16, Romans 5:12, 1 Peter 3:18). In this way, God knew that the world was in need of a savior (identifying the need), so God sent His son Jesus into the world that the world be saved through Him (meeting the need - 1 John 4:9). This fact is further revealed as Jesus responded to Zacchaeus by saying "the Son of Man came to seek and save those who are lost. (Luke 19:10, New Living Translation)." Furthermore, in John 20:21, Jesus declares, *"Peace be with you! As the Father has sent me, I am sending you."*

Why do some leaders have misconceptions about marketing?

To begin, I'm convinced that marketing misconceptions arise from a lack of understanding of marketing's definition, concepts, and methods. This lack of understanding has led some to dismiss this critical tool utilized by secular business executives to understand and meet the demands of their target customers. If Walmart, Amazon, and Target can use marketing to sell bottled water to their customers to fulfill a temporary thirst, how much more should the church capitalize on marketing to offer Jesus, who declared, "Those who drink of the water I give will never thirst again" (John 4:14, New Living Translation).

In Mark 16:15, Jesus commands his disciples to "Go into all the world and preach the gospel to all creation." This passage suggests that it is important to share the message of salvation with as many people as possible, and the principles of marketing, properly applied, can greatly aid this process. Similarly, in (Matthew 28:19-20), Jesus gives the Great Commission to his disciples, saying, "Go and make disciples of all nations, baptizing them in the name of the Father and of the Son and of the Holy Spirit, and teaching them to obey everything I have commanded you." This passage emphasizes the importance of spreading the message of faith. I submit that the principles of marketing shared in this book can help your church put the "right message" in front of the "right person" at the "right time." Next, some leaders equate marketing with questionable sales tactics." Like most, I, too, have been on the receiving end of an unscrupulous salesman who sold products with impressive packaging but only to find out later that I was a victim of bait and switch.

I believe this and other experiences have caused some leaders to stay away from marketing because they do not want to be associated with unethical sales practices.

According to Kotler and Keller's book, "Marketing Management," "The aim of marketing is to make selling superfluous." In other words, once you understand the needs of the target audience for your product or service, the product or service becomes a natural fit like a fine hand-crafted suit; it just fits! *As a side note.* I have seen church websites that display the church in a way that *may not* be the most accurate representation. In some cases, this is the result of designing the website with sample graphics available on the internet. This can be viewed negatively by attendees and most likely can impact their decision to return. Instead, when promoting the church on the web, be sure it reflects the makeup, model, and mission of the church as well as encapsulates the message of salvation through Jesus Christ.

Another common misconception is that "advertising encompasses marketing as a whole". On the contrary, while advertising or promotion is a component of marketing, it is not the total sum of marketing. To properly encapsulate marketing, emphasis must be placed on all the "P's of marketing." E. Jerome McCarthy was the first person to suggest that marketing is far broader than just advertising. McCarthy suggested that there are 4 P's that comprise the marketing mix, which are the product, the price, the place, and the promotion. In this book, I will go into detail on the 4 P's of marketing as well as expand my definition of marketing to include a fifth P, "prayer," which is vital for a holistic and biblical approach to marketing.

Continuing, some reject marketing because the term "marketing" is not found in the Bible, and the assumption is that this concept is not biblical. The ultimate goal of church marketing is not to sell a product or service but to share the message of the gospel and bring people closer to God. For example, the Apostle Paul's approach to evangelism can be clearly seen as a form of marketing. He understood the needs and desires of his audience, adapted his message to meet their needs and expectations, and effectively communicated the gospel to them. In his letter to the Corinthians, he says, "To the weak I became weak, to win the weak. I have become all things to all people so that by all possible means I might save some" (1 Corinthians 9:22 New International Version).

As a side note, if you perform a cursory examination of the words we use today and their associated practices, there are quite a few things that are readily accepted by the church that do not find their origin in the scripture. One word that comes to mind, which may have something to do with the time of year I am writing this book, is Christmas. Christmas is celebrated by Christians and non-Christians alike. If you were like me, you told your young children the story of a man in a red suit with a bunch of reindeer who one day will make his way down the chimney to deliver gifts.

Now, there are many reasons why Christians have made the decision to hold on to this story, but what does remain true is that our Savior was born to save the world from their sins, and this fact, which was celebrated by the wise men (Matthew 2:1-2, 11) should still be celebrated today. We all agree that Christmas is highly commercialized, and the focus of the business sector is not our risen Savior. The business sector uses a time that should be set aside to celebrate the birth of our Savior to make substantial profits.

As a matter of fact, Black Friday, which occurs the day after Thanksgiving, was said to be the day of the year when businesses begin to turn a profit, going from a red or unprofitable state to a black or profitable state. Just as the business sector has decided to use marketing for the purpose of making a corporate profit, I suggest that the church explore how marketing concepts and principles can assist in presenting the Gospel of Christ to their community.

Additionally, just because some have decided to use marketing for bad purposes and thereby giving it a bad name does not mean that the church should abandon it. On the contrary, I believe the church should show the world what marketing looks like when it is done for the purpose of presenting God's gift (Jesus) to a world who is in desperate need of His love, His life, and His Lordship.

The final misconception that I would like to address is that "marketing is a waste of money." As I stated previously, the typical return on investment for a successful marketing campaign is estimated to be 400%, with some campaigns yielding even higher returns of 900%. With these numbers in mind, it is possible for the church to experience similar positive outcomes by implementing effective marketing strategies. These marketing and outreach initiatives can assist churches in bringing in more frequent visitors, attracting new members, and engaging their communities in fresh and new ways.

The list of things that are marketed is vast and includes:

1. Goods like cars, houses, food, and toys.

2. Services like barbering, doctors, lawyers, and tax preparation.

3. Experiences like a Disney vacation or a family cruise.

4. Information like "How to pay off your credit cards in 30 days?"

5. Events like an ad regarding the hottest gospel singer coming to your town

Interestingly, everything on the list of "things marketed" above is temporal and has no eternal value. The church is the only organization that can offer the "One" who provides lasting peace and eternal life. After reading this book, I hope that more leaders believe that using marketing to share the life, the love, and the liberty provided by Jesus Christ is worth it.

Church marketing is not about simply telling people what they want to hear. Instead, it involves meeting people where they are, empathizing with their struggles, and offering the only true solution to their problems - Jesus Christ. By connecting with people in a meaningful way and sharing the message of salvation through Jesus, churches can reach those who are searching for hope and meaning in their lives. My aim in writing this book is to make a case for the use of marketing within the church to ultimately help churches reach their community and impact the lives of those whom God has entrusted to their care.

Chapter 3

The Church

Now, let us look at some trends that have affected or impacted the church over the years. According to the Hartford Institute for Religion Research, there are approximately 350,000 churches in existence today in the United States, with over 56 million worshipers in attendance each week. A 2014 church survey estimated that out of the 350,000 existing churches, over 10,000 will close their doors each year. The Barna Group reports that the average size of a congregation in America is 89 adults, and with every church closing, there are about 100 congregants who are left without a spiritual covering. The Barna Group further stated that there are 50 percent fewer churches today compared to 100 years ago, and on average, 3,500 people leave the church on a daily basis. Compared to the rapid growth of the United States population, the percentage of the population attending church has fallen significantly since 1950.

Interestingly, Jeff Haynes, in his book "Religion in Global Politics," shared that "scholars have proposed that churches have declined in power and prominence in most industrialized societies, except in cases in which religion serves some function in society beyond merely regulating the relationship between individuals and God." In an Association of Religion Data Archives (ARDA) survey, 56 percent of the people surveyed stated that religion as a whole is losing its influence in America, while 37 percent felt religious influence was increasing.

According to an Akron Beacon Journal article entitled, "'Difficult days are ahead' for America's churches, faith institutions," "nearly 70% of Americans identify as Christian, but just one in three attends worship services on a consistent basis. In a 2023 survey conducted by Churchtrack, 20% of Americans attend church on a weekly basis, 41% attend monthly, while 57% say they seldom or never attend religious services. Lastly, the survey concludes that regular church attendance has steadily declined since the turn of the century.

In contrast, people who claim no religious affiliation are one of the fastest-growing groups in the United States". Additionally, Gallup asked U.S. adults who do not have a religious affiliation whether they are interested in exploring religion in the future. The vast majority -- 75% -- say they are "not interested at all," while 13% indicate they are "a little interested," 9% "moderately interested" and 3% "very interested.

. As church attendance declines, there are fewer

people who hear the gospel, fewer people are engaged in a loving relationship with Jesus through the local church, fewer people who are available to help spread the gospel, and fewer people to help sustain the mission and ministry of the local church. Should church leaders be concerned with the decline in church attendance? Does it matter if the Christian church's attendance is declining? Moreover, is church attendance a good indicator of the health and success of a church?

I believe church attendance is an important measure because it represents believers who have found the message of Jesus Christ to be so important that they are willing to give up their time, talent, and treasure in support of their local church. Moreover, I believe church attendance is not the only measure of church health, but it is an important measure that should be considered among other measures.

The Churched vs. Unchurched

According to a 2020 Gallup poll, 47% of Americans say they belong to a house of worship, down by 3% from a 2018 survey. Interestingly, U.S. church membership was as high as 73% of the population when Gallup first measured it in 1937 and remained near 70% for the next six decades. In the last two decades, church attendance has dropped 26%, which equates to 85 million fewer Americans attending church.

As of 2014, there were 318 million people living in the United States of America. Out of that number, 162 million have attended at least one church service in the previous six months. That leaves approximately 156 million, or 49 percent of all people living in America, to be classified as churchless or unchurched. This is mainly because they have not attended a church service in the last six months, excluding special events like funerals or weddings. In the article "10 Facts about America's Churchless", Barna shares the following facts:

- As of 2014, the estimated number of people in the U.S. who Barna Group would define as "churchless"— meaning they have not attended a Christian church service, other than a special event such as a wedding or a funeral, at any time during the past six months— stands at 114 million. Add to that the roughly 42 million children and teenagers who are unchurched, and you have 156 million U.S. residents who are not engaged with a Christian church.
- "If all of the unchurched people were a separate nation, they would comprise the eighth most populous country in the world, trailing only China, India, Indonesia, Brazil, Pakistan, Bangladesh."
- "The generational composition of the churched and the unchurched is very similar. The makeup of the churched population is "Millennials make up 11%, Generation X at

33%, the Baby Boomers make up 35%, and the Silent generation makes up the remaining 22%". However, the unchurched percentages are a little lower; "Millennials make up 15%, Generation X make up 36%, the Baby Boomers are 33%, and the Silent generation make up the remaining 16%".

- When asked to identify their faith beliefs, 62% of unchurched adults consider themselves Christians. Most of the churchless in America—contrary to what one might believe—do not disdain Christianity nor desire to belittle it or tear it down. Many of them remain culturally tied to Christianity and are significantly interested in it.

- The majority of unchurched individuals (76%) have firsthand experience with one or more Christian churches and, based on that sampling, have decided they can better use their time in other ways.

- Among the unchurched, less than half (44%) are married, while the number is closer to six out of 10 among the churched. A greater proportion of the unchurched (29%) than the churched (22%) has never been married. Unchurched adults are also about four times more likely to be cohabiting than the churched (11% and 3%, respectively). Both groups are equally likely to be divorced, separated, or widowed.

The Mission of the Church

Like other organizations, it is the role of the organization's founder to craft and communicate the mission for which the organization was started. In the same way, Jesus shared the mission of the church in the book of Matthew.

Jesus stated, "All authority in heaven and on earth has been given to me. Therefore, go and make disciples of all nations, baptizing them in the name of the Father and of the Son and of the Holy Spirit, and teaching them to obey everything I have commanded you" (Matthew 28:18-20 New International Version). This text reveals that the church's mission is to take the Gospel to the world.

Church leaders must be vigilant and constantly assess how well they are carrying out this responsibility both for the church as a whole and as individual Christians. The mission of the church springs from the heart of God and his love for mankind. This is clearly shown in John 3:16 which states, "For God loved the world so much that he gave his one and only Son so that everyone who believes in Him will not perish but have eternal life" (John 3:16, New Living Translation).

God's love for the lost is further solidified in the three parables of the lost coin, the lost sheep, and the lost son, found in Luke 15. Also known as "The Lost Trilogy,"

Luke 15 is a revelation of the love of God towards the lost, a reflection of the mission of Christ to save the lost, and a reminder of the work of the church to reach the lost. For Jesus stated the reason why He came in Luke 19, "For the Son of Man came to seek and save those who are lost." Then, in the gospel of John, Jesus says, "As the Father sent me, I am sending you" (John 20:21 New International Version).

I believe each church's leadership should determine what role their church will play in bringing about the mission of the Church for the community that God has allowed them to serve. Understandably, every church will not be able to spread the Gospel to all nations, but to actively and effectively reach the people within your neighborhood and your city for Christ may be your church's fulfillment of the mission that Christ gave to the church.

Chapter 4

The Organizational Life Cycle of the Church

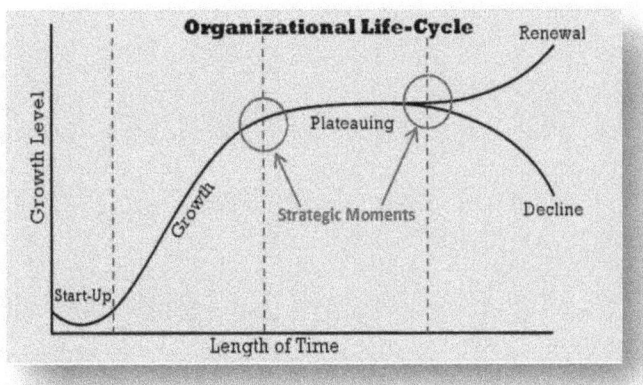

Figure 1. Organizational life cycle

Just like other organizations, churches experience different stages or cycles throughout their lifespan. Similar to how organisms are born, grow, mature, decline, and eventually die, churches go through a similar cycle.

Churches are established, grow, and reach a plateau, and eventually decline either upon achieving their objectives or due to other factors. Thus, the organizational life cycle outlines the various phases that an organization progresses through, starting from its inception until its eventual dissolution. Startup, growth, plateau, renewal, and decline are the 5 stages of an organization's life cycle. It is crucial for leaders to understand the organizational life cycle and know which stage of the life cycle their church is in to build a healthy and vibrant church.

Organizational Life-Cycle Phases

Start-Up:

The first stage of the Organizational life cycle is the start-up phase. During this phase, the planning and launching of the church occur.

The church leader and the core group of individuals sense a deep conviction to start a new church, usually driven by a desire to meet specific spiritual needs within a particular community or demographic. Once the startup phase progresses, the church prepares for its official launch or opening. This phase is an exciting and pivotal time for a church, as it sets the foundation for its future growth and impact.

This phase requires strong leadership, a clear vision, strategic planning, and a dedicated team of individuals who are passionate about building a thriving church community. Since the goal of this book is not to start a church but rather to market a church, I recommend visiting StartChurch.com for assistance with starting your church. StartChurch.com is dedicated to serving church planters by helping them get started on the right legal foundation, ensuring every church planter can protect what God has called them to lead. Start Church helps to relieve the administrative burden associated with starting and establishing a church.

Growth:

The growth stage proceeds to the startup stage and can last several years as the church is new and fresh to its congregants. This stage is when the church becomes more stable and continues to increase the number of staff and members. During this stage, discipleship programs are established to ensure the spiritual health of the church. Baptisms and baby christenings are frequent as new members join and begin to connect.

The growth stage is typically very exciting for the church, its staff, and its members. According to Pastor.com, the average church grows for 15 years, plateaus, and then declines and dies, but this is not true of every church. Some churches have longer growth spans, others have shorter ones, and unfortunately, there are some churches that never experience substantial growth.

Plateauing:

The church typically enters a plateau, which is signified by the church membership attendance remaining constant as the church body matures. According to Thom S. Rainer, CEO and Founder of Church Answers, 65% of the churches in America find themselves either in a plateau or declining stage, while 35% are growing. Often, the plateauing is a result of changing demographics, leaders not being willing to commit to change, or a crisis moment that impacts the church and causes people to leave.

According to Rick Warren, founding Pastor of Saddleback Church, churches often plateau at 75 and 150 people, with the hardest plateaus to break being 300. Rick Warren believes if you can get past 300, you'll likely have solved many of your most difficult challenges because the church has developed the skills needed to get through the early growth and plateau cycles.

Regardless, it is important to recognize a plateau or a decline and take needed actions to curtail these stages and spawn a renewal. Monitoring the membership trending on a monthly and yearly basis can provide church leaders with the needed insight regarding which stage of the organization's life cycle the church is in so that appropriate actions can be taken. If the proper actions are taken, the church can enter a renewal stage and continue to grow. If no action or the wrong actions are taken, a decline in membership is inevitable.

Renewal:

The renewal phase is analogous to the growth stage and can be seen as the church gaining its second wind. During this phase, the church continues to grow numerically and mature spiritually. The renewal stage can last for several years and will almost always lead to the return of a plateau unless the church leadership continues to do those things necessary to continue to help the church grow.

Decline:

As you suspect, decline most certainly involves a decrease in the church's membership, staff departures, and, among other things, a decrease in giving. It's important to note that all organizations will decline if the proper steps are not taken to renew the organization. Take the example of Walmart and Kmart. At the time of the writing of this book, Walmart is the low-price leader and is the 15th largest company in the US by market capitalization.

Conversely, Kmart, which once operated over 2,486 stores globally, today only has 17 Kmart branded stores and an online website that has 2.4 million visits per day vs. Walmart's 563 million visits per day. For all intents and purposes, Kmart is no longer a competitor in this space. Churches are not exempt from decline, and although Jesus, in a conversation with Peter, stated that the gates of hell will not conquer the Church at large (Matthew 18:16 New Living

Translation), individual churches will suffer decline if not attended to.

Finally, it's crucial to have the insight to discern where your church stands in its life cycle. With this understanding, you will have the needed information to take the necessary steps to move forward. This balance between renewal and stability enables churches to adapt, grow, and effectively navigate the evolving needs of their congregation and the broader community they serve.

Assess Reasons for Your Church's Organizational Life Cycle Phase

What should church leaders do with the knowledge of the Organizational Life Cycle? After understanding where your church is relative to the organizational lifecycle, it is good to review your strategic plan to understand how and why the church is in a particular phase. You can recall from the earlier chapters that the contents of a strategic plan will be different for each church but can include your mission or purpose statement, which states why the church exists, a vision statement detailing where the church hopes to go, objectives that measure progress towards the vision, a strategy, describing how to execute on objectives and core values that set the boundaries for how your church will pursue their vision and mission.

Having a strategic plan and knowing how well you are executing is critical for a healthy and growing church. To know how well you are executing your strategic plan, you need to measure and evaluate the performance of your church as a whole, as well as each individual department or ministry. As an example, students are given a test to see how well they are learning the prepared material. In turn, the test results are used to assess and improve the effectiveness of the educational program. This produces a strategic circle where performance is tested for effectiveness, and this effectiveness is used to modify the strategic plan.

The strategic plan of a church should be flexible and adaptable, allowing for adjustments as the church's needs and external factors evolve. The plan should be regularly reviewed, refined, and revised to ensure its relevance and effectiveness in guiding the church's growth and impact.

A good tool used to evaluate the church as a whole or a particular ministry against the strategic plan is the SWOT analysis. The acronym SWOT stands for Strengths, Weaknesses, Opportunities, and Threats. During the strength evaluation, you will ask, "What are we doing well as a church or as a ministry?" Weaknesses refer to what we can do better or what we need to improve. Both strengths and weakness refer to the internal condition of your church and, most importantly, things that you can do something about.

Conversely, opportunities and threats deal with the external conditions that your church can take advantage of to help in its growth and vitality, as well as the threats that can negatively impact your church yet are outside of your church's control. One example of an external threat that started in January 2020 was the COVID-19 pandemic. Many churches closed their doors as a result, yet other churches changed their ministry model to adapt.

When conducting a SWOT analysis, it's always good to start with your church's strengths to highlight what the church does well. When considering what your church does well, I would suggest refraining from comparing your church against other churches but rather using your strategic plan as your starting point for comparing where your church is relative to where you hoped it would be.

As you start the SWOT analysis, don't anticipate perfection, especially when creating a church SWOT analysis for the first time. You will make errors, and you will take away lessons from them, but it will get better with each SWOT analysis. The biggest barrier to doing SWOT analyses, in my experience, is understanding and acknowledging organizational weaknesses. No one wants to talk about weaknesses.

Any organization conducting a SWOT analysis should seek to be honest about its weaknesses. If an organization can't look truthfully at its existing weaknesses, a SWOT analysis would be meaningless. The church will need to understand why a particular weakness exists and work to either eliminate it or turn the weakness into a strength.

Dr. Brandon Pardekooper of the Ministry Hackers has a YouTube video that gives a great explanation of the SWOT analysis and how your church can make the best use of it. Simply search the Ministry Hackers on YouTube and select the video entitled, *"How to Assess Your Church Using SWOT?"*

Need More Help?

If your church needs assistance understanding and progressing through the various life-cycle stages, may I suggest that companies like "The Unstuck Group" @ www.theunstuckgroup.com or Artistry Labs @ www.artistrylabs.com. These companies are positioned to help churches understand their current stage of the life cycle and design a plan to help move the church to the next level.

Chapter 5

The Strategic Plan

It is important for the church leadership to understand, document, and disseminate a strategic plan setting the short-term, long-term, and overall direction of the church before developing a marketing strategy.

Of course, even before developing a strategic plan, the church leadership should first solidify the mission of that individual church. Solomon stated, "Many are the plans in a person's heart, but it is the Lord's purpose that prevails" (Proverbs 19:21 New International Version). In other words, without God's directions, the best-laid plans are fruitless.

The contents of a strategic plan will be different for each church but can include a mission or purpose statement that states why the church exists, a vision statement detailing where the church hopes to go, objectives that detail and measure progress towards the vision, a strategy describing how to execute on objectives, core values that set the boundaries for how to pursue the vision and mission, and lastly methods to monitor progress and initiate corrective adjustments.

It is essential that a church's strategic plan pass the

fit test. The fit test determines how well the congregation, the leadership, and the resources and capabilities of the church match with the strategic plan. In other words, a church's strategic plan should be focused on achieving objectives that fit the organization's capabilities.

For example, a church with a strategic plan to reach a younger audience but lacks the consensus of the leadership and congregants to make and accept the change may fail due to a lack of strategic fit. Implementing a change strategy that drastically affects or seeks to alter the culture or makeup of the church should be done with care and much prayer. Since changing a church's culture is not an easy task and can take about 3 to 5 years to accomplish, this strategy should only be pursued if the leadership is absolutely up for the challenge and in for the long haul.

Effective Strategic Planning Includes the Following:

- Reflecting the organization's values and principles.
- Clearly identify the critical factors for success.
- Ensuring that everyone is focused and moving in the same direction.
- Encourage the use of strategies effectively.

The Mission

Why Does the Church Exist?

The mission statement is the most important part of the strategic plan and is the fountain on which all else stands". First and foremost, the mission statement reveals "why your church exists." The mission statement is descriptive in nature, describes the purpose, and answers the question: Why do we exist?

The mission statement is generally comprised of two elements; "What is the church going to do?" and "For whom will the church do it." Typically, both the mission and vision statements are crafted by the senior leadership of the church, while the goals and objectives are the responsibility of departmental or ministry leaders and are used to explain each department or ministry's role in achieving the mission and vision of the church. Below are a few examples of church mission statements that can be used to validate or help prepare your church's mission.

North Point Community Church (Alpharetta, GA)

"To lead people into a growing relationship with Jesus Christ."

Victory Church (Norcross, GA)

"To develop fully committed disciple of Jesus."

Mars Hill (Seattle, WA)

"To plant churches and make disciples."

Seacoast Church (Mt Pleasant, SC)

"We exist to help people become fully devoted followers of Christ."

It's important for the church to have a clear and concise mission statement that guides its actions and priorities. The mission statement should be based on biblical principles and aligned with the vision of the church.

It should also be communicated effectively to the congregation so that everyone can work collectively towards fulfilling the mission.

The Vision

What Are We Striving to Be?

A vision is a mental image of a possible or desirable future state. The vision should work to paint a picture of the long-term desires of the church. The vision should be aspirational, forward-looking, and directional and help to keep the church and its leadership focused on the course ahead. The vision should also be flexible and adjustable as the church leadership continues to seek God for clarity.

Once the vision is crafted, the essence of the vision

should be encapsulated in an easy-to-remember slogan, which helps church members and leadership easily internalize, remember, and recite the vision as a reminder of the course ahead.

Below are a few examples of church or corporate vision statements that can be used to validate or prepare your church's vision. Examples:

North Point Community Church (Alpharetta, GA)

"To be a church that unchurch people love to attend."

The Rock (San Diego, CA)

"To be a global and highly trusted model of relevant and innovative evangelism."

High Point Church (Memphis, TN)

"To be a place where LOVE WORKS."

Phoenix First (Phoenix, AZ)

"To be the church that displays the love of Christ and connects with people of all walks of life through our creative services, discipleship, outreach, and the establishment of multiple campuses by streaming our Weekend Experience services globally.[i]"

Walmart

"To be the destination for customers to save money, no matter how they want to shop."

The Objectives

How Are We Progressing?

Objectives serve the purpose of converting the church's vision and mission statements into specific performance targets. Objectives should be reflective of the church's leadership's aspirations relative to reaching the desired community in which the church resides, whether local, national, or international in scope. Moreover, objectives should be SMART, meaning that they should be specific, measurable, achievable, relevant, and time-based. Ensuring that objectives are SMART ensures that they are quantifiable and measurable and able to achieve a stated deadline.

Two common types of objectives important to the success of any church are financial and strategic. Financial objectives can include initiatives like raising funds to pay off or purchase a new building or vehicle or establishing a capital campaign aimed at increasing annual giving by a certain percentage. The importance of a church reaching its financial objectives is obvious, without which the church's very existence is at risk. Conversely, strategic objectives are goals related to the execution of the church's organizational strategy.

Strategic objectives can include items like growing the church by a certain percentage and increasing church participation in local outreach by a certain percentage. Objectives can be short-term (three to six months) and or long-term (three to five years). Also, objectives should exist at every ministry or department level of the church and must support rather than conflict or negate the overall financial and strategic goals of the church. The accomplishment of a church's strategic and financial objectives is an important indicator that the church is well- positioned to accomplish its mission and vision.

The Strategy

How to Execute Objectives?

While the vision seeks to inspire, the strategy serves as a guide. Churches often know where God is calling them, but how God is directing them to get there is not always as clear. To this end, strategy can mean many things, but in the context of this chapter, strategy is a set of activities or tasks aimed at guiding the church to achieve its objectives. A strategy should exist for each organizational level of the church. The top-most level of a church's strategy is considered the "Organizational Level," while lower-level strategies are considered "Supportive."

It is also possible for an organization to have both a supportive strategy that supports the overall vision of the church and an organizational strategy that guides the achievement of the objectives for a particular subset of the organization.

Dr. Garland Vance, CEO and Founder of Advance Leadership, provided 4 organizational-level strategies that a church can pursue:

1. Church Growth Strategy: This strategy deals with the numerical growth of the church. Does the church focus on growing the local church, launching a new campus, or increasing internet outreach?

2. Community Engagement Strategy: This strategy can include which neighborhood, location, and people or group your church desires to reach, as well as the methods by which you will reach them.

3. Leadership Strategy: This strategy can include how your church will identify, develop, and mobilize leaders.

4. Personal Spiritual Growth Strategy: This strategy can include how to develop and support the personal spiritual growth of those that your church has decided to reach and teach.

The Core Values

What Guides Our Pursuit?

Core values are the beliefs, traits, and behavioral norms that guide the church's pursuit of its vision and mission. Core values can also be thought of as the description of the church's culture and the manner in which its members conduct themselves. I have listed below the core values of Watermark Community Church, which I believe is both a great list of core values as well as an example of well-thought-out principles to guide any ministry.

Watermark Community Church (Dallas, Tx)

OUR CORE VALUES

We unashamedly and uncompromisingly strive to be:

Biblically Based:

God's Word is our guide, authority, and conscience in everything. We stand firm where it stands firm and remain flexible where it is flexible. (2 Timothy 3:16)

Fully Devoted to Christ:

We measure our success by our ability to be and make disciples. Full devotion to Jesus is normal for every believer. (Luke 9:23)

Rounded In Grace:

We acknowledge our complete dependence on the goodness and grace of God. We have benefited from the kind intention of His will; therefore, we eagerly extend it to others. (Ephesians 2:8-9)

Passionate About Prayer:

We believe the attitude and action of prayer are essential to everything we do. (Colossians 4:2)

Authentic in Our Walk:

Authenticity, integrity, openness, and sincerity will define us. "The goal of our instruction is love, from a good conscience, a pure heart, and a sincere faith." (1 Timothy 1:5)

Committed to the Uncommitted:

We believe that lost people matter to God; therefore, they matter to us. Jesus came to seek and save the lost and has left us here, in part, to do the same. Our individual lives and corporate efforts will reflect this conviction. (Luke 19:10)

Relevant and Innovative:

The Bible does not tell us to use only certain styles of music or to present our message only through words. The Bible does make it clear, however, that we are to find ways to effectively bring the message *"into all the world"* to make disciples. We believe this will require scrutiny of everything we do - new practices and old - and a willingness to change, when necessary, within biblical parameters, in order that we, "by all possible means might save some." (1 Corinthians 9:22)

Committed To Community:

Belonging to our community requires a commitment to being intentionally involved with others in accountable, encouraging relationships. We believe life change happens best in the context of relationships. In clusters of caring people, participants share and encourage each other toward spiritual growth.

Here, people can experience both the benefits of a larger church and enjoy the kind of relationships that only develop in small, safe settings. (Hebrews 10:24-25)

Focused on Ministry and Service:

We believe that each believer has received a special gift and should employ it in serving others as good stewards of the manifold grace of God. Spiritual giftedness and maturity determine where and how a believer serves. We believe excellence honors God and reflects His character. We strive for excellence without compromise in all areas of our ministry and lives[ii]. (1 Peter 4:10; Colossians 3:17)

Measuring the Impact

How Do We Track Progress?

I have worked in the information technology industry for over 20 years. Two statements that I commonly hear are, *"What gets measured matters"* and *"What gets measured gets done."*

I'm not sure how common these statements are in most churches, but I believe these statements still ring true. It is important for church organizations to understand how well they are carrying out their mission.

Key performance indicators (KPIs) are measurable values used to determine how effectively an organization is achieving its key performance objectives (KPIs). Stephen Blandino, in his article "The Six Metrics of Church Health," provides some well-thought-out metrics that churches can use to measure and monitor their health.

1. **Audience:** Who are we reaching?

2. **Stories:** Are lives being changed?

3. **People:** Are we developing disciples and leaders?

4. **Numbers:** Are we growing?

5. **Movement:** Are we trending forward?

6. **Culture:** Is our environment healthy?

This is not a comprehensive list of metrics, nor will all these metrics be appropriate for all churches. But I believe measuring the performance of your church is a part of being a good steward. Of course, numbers do not tell the whole story because some things are not measurable. For instance, the transformation of the heart or an individual's level of spirituality are things that should not and cannot be measured with metrics.

Conversely, there are many things that can and should be measured to understand if the church is fulfilling its mission, blossoming into its vision, and being a good steward of what God has entrusted. But remember, as Proverbs 27:23 reminds us, "Be diligent to know the state of your flocks and attend to your herds." This verse highlights that church leaders should know the state of their church and the people and must be attentive to its growth and well-being, which is essential in fulfilling the Church's vision and mission.

Chapter 6

Markets and Marketing

What are Markets?

A market is a physical or virtual place where those who desire to buy or transact interact with those who desire to sell. The term market can also be specific segments or groups of customers, constituents, or congregants that a company, government, or church targets with its products or services. These markets are defined based on various characteristics that include demographic, geographic, psychographic, or behavioral factors. For example, the housing market refers to a group of buyers and sellers who seek to transact homes.

The Need for Markets

Markets are essential for several reasons:

- They facilitate the exchange of goods and services, whether through bartering or monetary transactions.
- Markets help in balancing the demand and supply of products through the price.

- They contribute to improving the overall quality of life in society by providing access to a wide range of goods and services.
- Markets serve as platforms for introducing new lifestyles, ideas, and innovations.
- They drive the development of products by targeting specific market segments and meeting diverse consumer needs.
- Markets play a crucial role in economic systems by promoting efficiency, innovation, and societal progress.

The Marketing Concept

Marketing is the process of promoting, selling, and delivering products or services to customers. Philip Kotler, often referred to as the father of modern marketing, defines marketing as "the science and art of exploring, creating, and delivering value to satisfy the needs of a target market at a profit." He emphasizes the importance of understanding customer needs and desires, creating value through products or services, and effectively delivering them to the target market.

Of course, the church is a part of the nonprofit religious market, which is comprised of organizations that seek to further social or religious causes or share a point of view. Obviously, nonprofit organizations are characterized by their tax-exempt status, which exempts them from paying taxes on money received. For the church, a market can be your church members, your community (whether virtual or physical), or a place where the church desires to interact with those with whom they wish to reach. The marketing environment of churches encompasses the external factors and influences that impact their outreach, engagement, and overall effectiveness in fulfilling their mission. These factors can include social, cultural, technological, economic, and competitive elements that shape the church's relationship with its congregation and the broader community.

The Power of Modern Marketing

According to the modern perspective, marketing is not just a separate function within a business; it is a fundamental aspect that encompasses the entire organization from the customers' perspective. Customers, not producers, determine whether a corporation succeeds. In this context, marketing is seen as a comprehensive strategy that places customers first and values their needs and preferences first. Consequently, customers are regarded as "key" in this modern concept of marketing. For the church, a customer-centered focus is not common. The central focus of the church is Jesus Christ, who is the author and founder of the church. Consequently, church marketing acknowledges that Jesus Christ is the central focus, but the unbeliever or unchurch should be the main focus of the church's marketing efforts.

Traditional Vs. Digital Marketing

The major difference between traditional and digital marketing lies in the channels and approaches used to reach the audience. While traditional marketing has a broader reach but limited interactivity, digital marketing takes advantage of the internet and technology to create more targeted, personalized, and interactive experiences for consumers. It embraces the digital landscape and the changing consumer behaviors and preferences in the digital era. Digital marketing uses the concept of micro-targeting to provide a better understanding of customer needs to position products or services more precisely in the minds of the customers or target audience. Retargeting is another digital marketing concept to reengage those who previously visited your website or social media page.

Word-of-Mouth (WOM) Marketing:

Word of mouth marketing (WOM), though seemingly simple, is often underestimated as a crucial component of a robust marketing strategy. When executed properly, WOM can be one of the most potent and cost-effective resources at your disposal. It relies on people sharing their positive experiences, which has a way of prompting others to try the product or service. A Nielsen study highlights that an astounding 92% of individuals trust recommendations from friends and family more than any other form of promotion.

Your congregation is the most passionate and capable extension of your marketing effort. Invite cards are a great resource to make it simple for members to invite others to the church and can be used as a conversation starter, thereby opening the way for them to share their experiences with others. Also, the Christmas season can be a catalyst for word-of-mouth promotion within the church community and can have a remarkable impact.

Christmas, as well as other holidays, naturally lends itself to sharing experiences and spreading goodwill. Encourage your congregation to share meaningful Christmas moments and invite friends and family to join festive worship services. This way, the church can harness the power of WOM to effectively convey its message and create a positive ripple effect throughout the community. Just as WOM can be used to share great news, negative information about your church and the visitor experience will travel fast. Just as your congregation will be passionate about extending good will about your church, visitors or disgruntled members will quickly share their negative experiences.

To head off any negative press, it would be good to include space on your welcome or connect card for visitors to share their experiences. You should ask visitors about their experience at your church and if they would consider returning, and if not, why not? This will provide you with the needed insight into how your service is being perceived and what changes your church should implement to make your church more welcoming. A follow-up call with a visitor who provided a negative comment may be just what is needed to overcome their negative experience and prompt them to consider returning. Also, including questions on your connect cards for visitors to share how they heard about your church will help to understand which marketing channels are effective and which are not. Lastly, adding a QR code to your connect cards allows visitors to provide their feedback directly from their smartphones.

Evolution of Markets and Marketing

Market and marketing evolution has been a fascinating journey that highlights the remarkable advancement and change seen throughout history. The development of markets, from their modest origins to the dynamic and linked digital systems we see today, reflects the continuously shifting needs and aspirations of society. Markets in the past were small-scale and unsophisticated, based on localized bartering and trade between nearby residents.

The idea of markets evolved when people were gathered to trade needed goods. These early marketplaces provided the basis for personal contact, economic activity, and interdependence among individuals. As civilizations rose, markets expanded, and trade routes were established, connecting distant regions and facilitating the exchange of goods and ideas. Markets became bustling hubs of economic activity, attracting sellers and buyers from far and wide.

In the era of modernization, the digital revolution has transformed markets once again. The rise of the internet and information technology has shattered physical barriers, enabling e-commerce and the globalization of markets. Online platforms have revolutionized the way we buy and sell, making transactions faster, more convenient, and accessible to a global customer base. The evolution of markets has brought about new business models, such as the sharing economy and digital marketplaces, creating opportunities for individuals and entrepreneurs to connect and engage in economic activities.

Today, markets have become highly sophisticated and interconnected ecosystems. They are influenced by numerous factors, such as consumer preferences, technological advancements, economic policies, and social trends. The evolution of markets has not only shaped the way we engage in business but also impacted social dynamics, cultural exchange, and the overall development of societies.

The evolution of markets is a testament to human ingenuity, adaptability, and the pursuit of progress. It reflects our ability to create systems that facilitate trade, enable innovation, and cater to the diverse needs of individuals. Lastly, as we reflect on how marketing has evolved, it is encouraging to consider the possibilities that the church has at its disposal to reach its community to the Glory of God.

Market Research

It's a good idea to conduct market research before starting any church marketing initiative. Market research allows the church to offer relevant programs or services since it provides a clear understanding of its member's or prospective members' needs or desires.

Market research helps churches gain insights into various factors that can impact the success of the church, including:

- Understanding the potential interest of members in attending other churches.
- Staying informed about popular trends within the church community.
- Gaining an understanding of the demographics of churchgoers and their specific challenges.

- Determining the motivations that drive people to attend church.
- Assessing perceptions of different aspects of the church, such as sermons, hymns, and community events.

With the help of comprehensive market research, churches can gather valuable insights that inform their decision-making processes. Market research empowers churches to tailor their offerings to better meet the needs and expectations of members and non-members alike, resulting in increased engagement, satisfaction, and the overall growth of the church community.

Check out "Market Research for Churches: A Beginners Guide"
http://www.dearyoungperson.com/market-research-for-churches/ for assistance with your market research. Also, check out "The Barna Group" @ www.Barna.com for other great resources to begin your journey on researching trends and topics that may be important to your church and help better understand those whom your church is called to reach.

Market Orientation

Market orientation is a marketing approach that emerged in the mid-1950s, emphasizing the importance of customer needs and satisfaction. The concept of marketing orientation is rooted in a broader marketing concept, which advocates for businesses to consistently prioritize the needs and desires of their customers. At its core, market orientation revolves around customer focus, with a strong emphasis on understanding and meeting customer needs.

The core components of market orientation are customer sensing and customer satisfaction. Likewise, in the context of the church, market orientation refers to the application of strategies to effectively meet the spiritual and physical needs of individuals and engage with the community. If a church wants to expand its outreach and attract more attendees, a market orientation approach would be a good option for gathering community insights. It provides a significant framework for church growth by demonstrating how churches can effectively meet needs and fulfill the great commission.

In this framework, preaching or evangelism would prioritize the needs of unbelievers and the unchurched, presenting the word in a way that resonates with them, just as Jesus did during His ministry. When spreading the "Good News," churches should consider the needs, expectations, and aspirations of their target audience in order to effectively reach them and bring them into a loving relationship with Jesus Christ.

First-Impressions Marketing

First impression is a strategy that deploys greeters, ushers, parking lot attendants, and guest or visitor services to create a welcoming environment for people visiting the church. Providing a warm reception, clear directions, comfortable seating, and other necessary materials contributes to making visitors feel welcome and increasing the likelihood that they will return. First impressions can be very important for your church because they empathize with first-time visitors and take into consideration their potential apprehensions.

Put yourself in the shoes of a first-time visitor and contemplate how your church can create a welcoming atmosphere. Are there parking lot attendants or clear signage that direct visitors to your church? Are there greeters at the front door, ready to greet visitors with warm smiles and kind greetings? Perhaps a welcoming gift can make them feel valued. Do you have ushers available to assist in finding comfortable seats or provide guidance to restrooms? Imagine how you would feel in their position, unfamiliar with the workings of a particular church, and then extend that consideration to your visitors.

By prioritizing a welcoming experience, you can foster a positive first impression that encourages visitors to feel at ease and embraced by your church community.

The Journey from the "Church Building" to "Church Online"

A noteworthy change in recent years has been the transition from attending the physical building to attending church online as digital platforms have become more widely available. For the church, this change has created both opportunities and challenges. Some people's decision to switch to online church is motivated by ease and flexibility. Online services enable people to participate in worship and spiritual activities while remaining at home and overcoming obstacles like distance, mobility challenges, or schedule conflicts.

It has also given those who would have been reluctant to visit a physical church another way to investigate and interact with the church. This change, though, has not been without difficulties. Online churchgoers miss out on the friendship, fellowship, and sense of physical presence that come with attending a regular church service. In a virtual environment, it is more difficult to make true connections and build a sense of belonging.

In the end, the transition from offline to online churchgoers is a reaction to the shifting dynamics of the contemporary world. It is evident that the traditional mass marketing approach is not as effective. This realization has led to the understanding that churches need to adapt and embrace a marketing strategy to assist in attracting new members. This point is emphasized in (Matthew 9:17), which speaks of putting new wine into new bottles to preserve both.

Accordingly, churches are encouraged to change the container in which they are presented. This implies that churches should innovate and adapt methods of reaching out to the younger generation, who have distinct preferences and expectations when it comes to church services. By adopting a marketing mindset and embracing new approaches, churches can effectively communicate their message and connect with potential members in a way that resonates with them.

How has the Church Market Changed?

In the past few years, there have been substantial changes in the church ministry (market) landscape. Church leaders have realized the need to streamline and condense their services to accommodate people's reduced attention spans and church-going weariness. Church leaders are aware that some of their internet viewers can be brand-new or regular viewers. Many churches have come to understand the importance of continuing to livestream their services to maintain a digital presence to reach far and wide even while they continue to meet in person.

With the widespread usage of social media, a staggering 4.7 billion people are actively engaged on these platforms worldwide. This presents churches with a remarkable opportunity to connect with individuals through social media communication. The question remains unanswered:

"Are churches effectively leveraging this social media potential?"

According to Lifeway Research, an astounding 85% of churches use Facebook as a social media platform. Additionally, 15% of churches utilize Twitter, while another 15% engage with their audience through Instagram. While maintaining an active presence on Faccbook is a wise choice, it is essential to recognize that other social media channels exist, offering the potential to reach an even larger audience.

To this end, I believe churches are recognizing the value of marketing and are allocating resources accordingly. Some church leaders clearly understand the importance of using marketing to reach their communities, promote their programs and events, and engage with both existing and potential members. While it is true that many churches may have limited or no budgets allocated specifically for marketing purposes, this appears to be a changing trend. Although it is recommended to allocate 5% to 10% of the church's annual budget to marketing, the actual available budget purposed for marketing can vary depending on several factors, including the size of the congregation, the financial resources available, and the overall priorities and strategies of the church leadership.

According to a survey conducted by the Unstuck Group, a significant portion of church budgets, specifically 52%, is allocated to staffing expenses such as salaries, benefits, and payroll taxes. Additionally, an average of 17% of the budget is dedicated to buildings and facility-related costs.

As a result, churches are utilizing approximately 69% of their budget for staff and facilities, leaving less than one-third of the budget for crucial areas like ministry programs, outreach initiatives, other essential expenses, and marketing.

Segmenting Markets (STP)

It is not possible for a church to reach or serve everyone in their community. God wants all to come to HIM through his Son, Jesus Christ, but not all will come to HIM through your church. It will prove difficult for anyone church to meet the worship style, sermon style, religious preferences, and needs of all in their target area.

In a Saleforce.com article entitled, "Step up

Marketing Strategy with STP," STP (Segmenting, Targeting, and Positioning) is defined as a marketing model that refines who you market your products or services to and how. STP makes your marketing communications more focused, relevant, and personalized toward those you are trying to reach. Churches can use the STP model to ascertain which part of their community or city God is leading then to reach. As mentioned in Kotler & Keller's "Marketing Management" book, this strategy is the essence of strategic marketing.

First, segmenting is the process of understanding and grouping the community into distinct groups?" Targeting is the process of selecting which groups your church is best positioned to reach. Lastly, positioning is the process of determining how your church is planning to reach and meet the needs of the selected segments".

As an aside, the demographics of your church reflect those whom your church is actually positioned to attract. If your church is predominantly white, black, Hispanic, Asian, or multi-cultural, the reason for this is your church is positioned to attract these groups. STP is about being intentional in selecting the right methods, crafting the right message, and having the right mindset to pursue those whom God has placed on the heart of your church.

Market Segmentation

Market segmentation, as detailed in figure 2 below, is the process of apportioning those you desire to reach into smaller groups, allowing your church to develop products or services based on the demographics, psychographics, behavioral, or geographic for each specific group. A youth church, a contemporary service, and a multi-cultural church are all examples of STP at work.

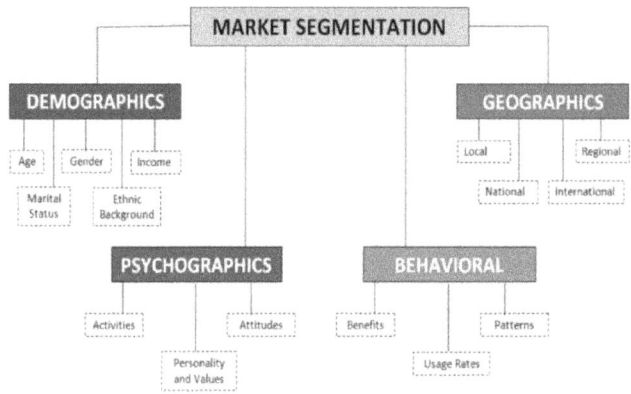

Figure 2: "How to use psychographics: The marketers guide."

By Alex Birkett, May 1, 2023.

As previously stated, since no one church can possibly meet the needs of everyone in their community, a decision should be made regarding how many and which segment(s) of the community the church desires to reach. The particular segment that the church decides to target should be reflected in the church's strategic plan and based on prayerful consideration.

A church must be very careful when targeting a segment of its community to avoid backlash. Incorrect targeting can generate public controversy if perceived as excluding vulnerable or disadvantaged groups or if targeting is perceived to exclude certain racial or ethnic groups.

Conversely, targeting improves the experience of those who attend because everything in the church is designed with them in mind. Who makes up our leadership team? What music should we sing? What sermon series should we select? What Biblical training should we schedule? Lastly, a church should be cognizant of the fact that there will always be those outside of the targeted areas who will choose to attend. They should be treated with respect and love, just like those who are in the targeted segments.

One of the first market segments that most churches will focus on is the geographical segment. This helps the church to determine the reach and scope of the ministry. Will the church be a community church and reach those within a 2-to-5-mile radius of the church? Or will the church instead only focus on the neighborhoods directly surrounding the church building because a 2-to-5-mile radius is too large for the church to effectively reach?

Interestingly, online streaming provides a church with another target market, which is outside of the church's geographical area. Some churches will assign a pastor to the online streaming church to cater to the needs of those who prefer not to visit the local church but who desire to participate virtually. The next market segment that a church may want to focus on is demographics.

Understanding the demographics of your target area is very important. For instance, if the demographics of your area are made up of families with young children, the church would need to tailor its ministries to focus on this very important characteristic. If a church fails to understand and is thereby unable to meet the needs of its target market, the church will be irrelevant to the people in that community; thereby, people won't come, and the church may not grow.

There are many market segments that a church may want to explore and position its ministry to serve. The last one that I will discuss is the psychographics segment. This is important when applied to whether a person is unchurched, unsaved, or churched. The needs of each of these groups are different and will require special consideration when promoting and crafting ministries to serve each group. For example, introducing controversial theological topics on a Sunday morning *may not* be the best thing for a church to present to those who are unsaved. These topics may be better suited for a bible study or training class, which will help lay the foundation for those first being introduced to Christ and who need a basic understanding of God and His love for them.

Chapter 7

The P's of Church Marketing

Jerome McCarthy developed the four Ps of marketing, also known as the marketing mix. These four P's; product, price, place, and promotion are foundational to the idea of marketing. For the church, "prayer," which is the fifth element of marketing, ensures that the other four Ps are properly positioned under the purview of the Most High.

In this way, prayer is the foundation on which the four Ps stand, and without prayer, the four Ps are simply a plan with no power, provision, or purpose. David declared that "the Lord knows all human plans; he knows that they are worthless (Psalms 94:11 New Living Translation)". Moreover, Proverbs 19:21 reveals that "many are the plans in a person's heart, but it is the Lord's purpose that prevails" (New International Version). Having prayer, the 5th P, as the foundation of your 4 P's ensures that God is the author of the purpose, plan, and pursuit of your church, and just like the ecclesia, is not of human design; "for upon this rock I will build my church and the gates of hell shall not prevail against it (Matthew 16:18 King James Version)"!

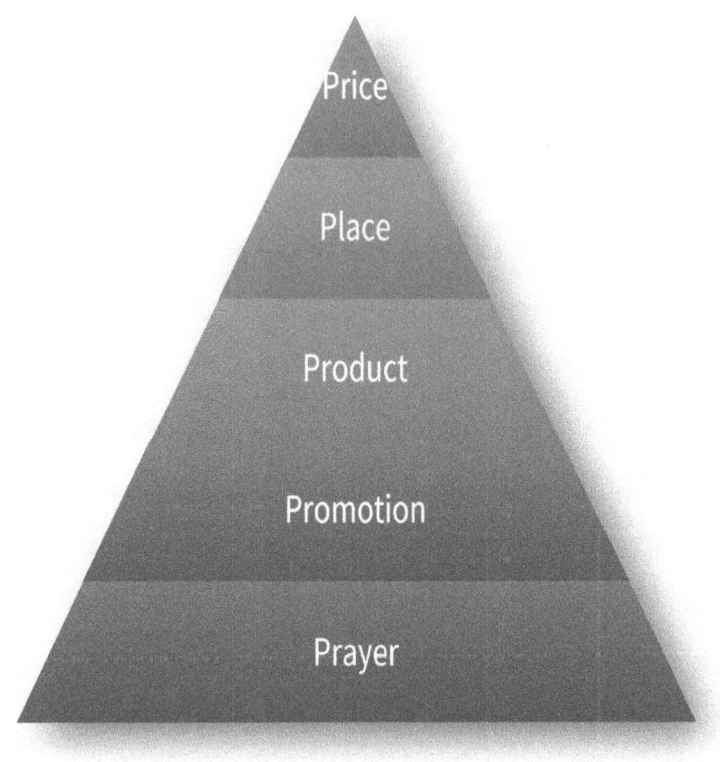

Figure 2. Five "P's" of Marketing

The Product

The product is the first "P" of church marketing. The product can be a tangible good or an intangible service produced to satisfy the needs of a certain or targeted group of people. Unlike the business community, the product produced by the church cannot exclusively be aimed at pleasing people, it must first be aimed at pleasing God.

Of course, the product produced by the church is starkly different than what is produced by the business community. It is important to note that the church is not trying to sell Jesus or salvation but is rather a conduit for building a relationship with Jesus and, ultimately, a way to partake of His wonderful gift of salvation. Some products produced by the church are the music, the message, the welcome, the walk-in, various teaching classes, and meaningful ways to connect with God and His people.

For the church, I believe the number one thing we should seek to produce is experience. Ultimately, the goal is for each person who comes to your church to have an experience with Jesus Christ. But the experience should start with a Google search for your church's website, Twitter, Instagram, YouTube, or Facebook page. The experience should continue upon arrival on the church property, from the parking lot to the door, from the door to the seat, and from the seat back to the parking lot. The question is, to whom should this experience be tailored? In his book, "Deep and Wide," Andy Stanley shares that the Northpoint churches tailor their experience to non-Christians.

Since statistically only 47 percent of the population regularly attend church on any given Sunday, tailoring the worship experience to include non-Christians provides the greatest opportunity to impact the Kingdom of God. Please understand that tailoring your church to non-Christians will require you to do things differently. Your website will have different content, your teaching and preaching will have a different focus, and your music will have a different target. These factors will be guided by the vision and mission of your church and the spiritual, physiological, and social needs of your church members and those whom you hope to attract.

Here are a few questions to help define your church's product: What music and service format will my church select? Traditional, contemporary, blended, or modern? What will be the sermon style? Expository, topical, textual, or sermon series? Do you preach to reach just the churched people in attendance, or do you target the sermon to reach the unchurched and unsaved as well? Focusing your church's product on the churched as well as the unchurched provides rich rewards, particularly as the unchurched are introduced to God for the first time, to experience His connection, to experience His touch, and ultimately to be led into a personal relationship with our Lord and Savior, Jesus Christ.

The Price

Price is the second "P" of the church marketing mix. Since most churches do not generate revenue from producing a core product or service, defining the price can be challenging. For the secular business, price represents the amount of money a consumer is willing to pay for a product or service. For the church, price represents both the tangible and intangible contributions one provides to become a member and maintain their church membership.

To this end, the price can be seen as the talent, time, and treasure that a person is willing to offer for the continuance of the church and its mission. The tithe and offering represent the treasure expected to be provided to the church by its members. For a believer who grew up in the church, the tithe is generally not considered a price but rather an act of worship.

For an unchurched person recently introduced to Christ who never has or is not accustomed to giving, paying a tithe or 10 percent of their income *"can"* be a roadblock. For example, let's take a new believer who receives and lives on a yearly salary of $100,000 per year. As a part of their new church membership, they are expected to freely give $10,000 per year. For some churches, this can also include a weekly offering, funds to support local church missions, as well as expectations to contribute money to the pastor and church anniversaries.

It is true that churches depend on the financial contributions of their members and visitors to continue operations. It is also true that giving 10 percent or the tithe is a biblical concept. But I would submit for some, giving financially *"can"* be a challenge. According to a 2023 Lending Club survey, 60 percent of Americans live from paycheck to paycheck, meaning, for these Americans, giving 10 percent is difficult. Moreover, according to a September 2023 Barna Group Survey, only 21 percent of all Christians give 10 percent of their income regularly.

In his book, "Deep and Wide', Andy Stanley tells new believers to start by picking a percentage they are willing and able to give and increase their percentage yearly. Andy suggests that selecting a percentage that works for the new believer helps them to transition to a place where they can begin to trust God financially.

This can help to expand their faith and move them to a place where money loses its grip and where they are no longer possessed by their possessions. Price can also represent the amount of time a person or family spends offering their talents and attending church. This can include bible studies, weekly meetings, weekday and weekend gatherings, choir rehearsals, local missions, community outreach, etc.

As a non-profit organization, churches depend on volunteers to help achieve their mission. It may be a good practice to ensure volunteers do not spend an inordinate amount of time at church. By suggesting a limit on the amount of time volunteers can spend on any given week as well as limiting the number of organizations a person can participate in, a church can build a healthy culture of volunteerism while helping to establish a good church-life balance among its members.

The Promotion

Promotion is the third "P' of the church marketing mix. When most people make a reference to marketing, promotion is what they often refer to. Also, most companies who are eager to help with your church's marketing efforts will mostly focus on advertising your church while neglecting to acknowledge the importance of the price, the place, and the products, which are vital to correctly positioning your church to reach its targeted community.

Promotion in ministry can also be called "needs-oriented selling." As a church, we recognize that the world is in need of a savior and that the church is the only organization that has the answer and the ability to meet this need. A church must effectively sell (share) the message of Jesus as the only answer to fill the need for salvation in their community. Individual ministries or departments have the need to promote as well.

The sound ministry needs technicians who are skilled in the art of sound reinforcement and are needed to help ensure that those in attendance can gain the faith necessary to receive the Lord Jesus Christ by providing clear, undistracted, and undistorted sound.

A church must effectively promote its products and services both internally and externally. Internally to its members to ensure that the church has the right resources to effectively staff ministries from those who currently attend and have the needed skills and passion to serve. Externally, to both effectively reach those in need of the message of Jesus Christ as well as those externally who have the skills needed to make ministry run effectively and would be willing to share their skills on a volunteer or pay-for-service basis.

Some churches will use their website for internal promotion by listing all the ministries available or in need of volunteers and often sharing this on the "connection" part of their website. In addition, some churches have periodic volunteer days where ministries can share their purpose and allow volunteers to sign up to help. This is important because a low level of engagement could mean people may not be excited about the church or that there is a 'Sunday only' mentality. This pattern may be a sign and can be associated with a decline in attendance, serving, or giving.

To this end, promotion includes advertising through various marketing channels. These marketing channels can include social media (Facebook, Instagram, Snapchat, YouTube, or Pinterest) or traditional media (websites, email, e-newsletters, postcard mailers, local TV, or radio).

Understanding and choosing the right marketing channel for the right message is important and maybe the difference between success and failure. Additionally, each channel is best suited for a particular "target audience," and using the right channel to reach the right audience is vital. Lastly, the content you are planning to share, whether text, video, or images, will likely dictate which platform is best for your message.

For example, if your church is hosting a "Senior Dance" for congregants 65 years old and older, Instagram would not be the best channel to choose for this promotion. With only a 13% utilization rate among seniors 65 years old and older, Instagram would not be your best choice to promote this event. Rather, Facebook, with a 50% utilization, or YouTube, with a 49% utilization rate, would be better platforms to target those 65 years old and older. Conversely, with a 95% utilization rate for groups 18 to 29, YouTube would be the right channel to reach this target group.

The Place

Place is the fourth "P" of the church marketing mix, also considered the distribution strategy. The role of the place is to distribute the product or service from the right location for it to be readily available for those targeted to consume it. Some of the places by which products can be distributed are the brick-and-mortar church, online or virtual church, door-to-door outreach, word-of-mouth outreach, as well as via social media websites like "TikTok," Instagram, and Facebook.

Location, location, location is still true when we talk about the places in which your church will engage its target audience. It is important to understand the role that "place" plays in delivering the services that your church offers to its community. Thanks to social media, your church can reach places that were not possible just a few years ago.

For example, a church in the great town of Lawrenceville, Georgia, can reach those in India, Africa, Mexico, China, or any place that has the internet capability to receive their services. This also opens opportunities for your church to reach and make a difference in the lives of people whom you would otherwise be unable to reach. Conversely, effectively reaching the places mentioned above will not just happen. The church will need to understand how the four "P's" of marketing are relative to that particular group and then effectively reach those groups. I think the best way of using the internet and social media is as an extension of your main church, specifically for members of your church who cannot attend on a particular Sunday or focused on those in the local area who would like to test your church online before entering the building.

Prayer

As you know, prayer is our direct connection to our Father and is foundational to the success of any church or its marketing or outreach effort. Solomon states in Proverbs 3:6, "Remember the Lord in all that you do, and He will give you success" (New Century Version). The main point here is any marketing, outreach, or evangelism plan must be Biblically based and prayerfully considered.

Additionally, Jesus said that we should seek the Kingdom of God above all else...and He will give you everything you need (Matthew 6:33 New Living Translation). In other words, seek God, then seek Him for what He wants to do in and through you and your ministry, and He will give you everything you need to do ministry. If your church doesn't have what it needs to reach your community, your target audience, or those around you, God can provide everything you need if you seek Him first. Do you want to know who you should reach in your community? Seek God First!

The Other P's of the Marketing Mix

While the traditional church marketing mix consists of the 5 Ps (Product, Price, Place, Promotion, and Prayer), there are additional Ps that can be relevant when considering marketing for a church. Here are some examples:

People:

The church's members are an essential part of its marketing efforts. This encompasses not only the clergy but also the devoted congregation, dedicated volunteers, and committed staff members.

It is crucial to prioritize nurturing meaningful connections, delivering exceptional service, and cultivating an inclusive and inviting atmosphere. Additionally, the church can showcase compelling narratives of people's personal transformation or share heartfelt testimonials to effectively demonstrate the profound and positive influence that God and the Church have had on people's lives.

Programs:

The diverse range of programs and ministries provided by the church contributes widely to its marketing mix. Church programs should cater to various age groups, interests, and community needs.

Effectively promoting these programs is essential to attract and engage both current and prospective members. In the case of a youth outreach program, the church can arrange captivating events like interactive workshops, engaging social activities, or meaningful community service projects. These initiatives can be strategically promoted through targeted channels such as social media platforms or local educational institutions.

Partnership:

Forming strategic partnerships with other churches, organizations, and community groups can bring significant value to a church's marketing efforts and extend its impact on the community. Both the church and the non-profit organization can combine their resources, whether it's volunteers, facilities, or financial contributions, to maximize their impact. For example, the church may offer its space for food distribution events, while the non-profit provides expertise in managing and coordinating the distribution process.

Working Through the 5 Ps of Church Marketing

The 5 Ps serve as valuable reference points for crafting a comprehensive marketing strategy. They provide guidance and can be revisited whenever needed, offering clarity and out-of-the-box thinking. Church marketing continues once people step through your doors. It's crucial to help first-time attendees to become regular attendees. Church marketing helps to craft plans to engage with first-time attendees after the service, have conversations, and extend a genuine invitation to come back.

As your church seeks to grow and impact the lives of those who live in your community, it is crucial to always keep this central truth at the heart of our efforts. We are not simply marketing a product or service; we are sharing something far more profound. We are introducing people to Jesus Christ, who came to proclaim good news to the poor, proclaim freedom for the prisoners, recovery of sight for the blind, and set the oppressed free (Luke 4:18-19 New International Version).

Chapter 8

Social Media Marketing

Today, social media platforms infiltrate every aspect of our lives. They have transformed how we interact with one another and have made it easier than ever to share our thoughts, emotions, and experiences with the rest of the world. A well-crafted social media marketing plan/strategy is essential for churches looking to engage with their members and the wider community, build a strong online presence, and share their message effectively. The key to success is to develop a clear understanding of your target audience, their needs, preferences, and the platforms they use most frequently. For churches, social media provides a unique opportunity to connect with members and non-members alike, share inspiring content, and promote events and activities. Creating relevant and engaging content that resonates with your audience fosters a sense of community, encourages engagement, and ultimately drives attendance and active participation.

Navigating the complex world of social media marketing for churches can be challenging, especially when you are new to marketing or unfamiliar with the latest trends and best practices. Some of the most popular social media platforms include Facebook, Twitter, Instagram, LinkedIn, TikTok, and YouTube. With very little effort, you can build connections with friends, family, and even strangers around the globe.

Defining Social Media Marketing

The origins of social media marketing can be found in the emergence of social media. Platforms like Myspace and Friendster came into existence in the early 2000s as places where users could connect with friends, share content, and engage in conversations over the internet. However, social media didn't truly start to take off until the 2004 launch of Facebook.

Soon, businesses started to realize the potential for marketing on Facebook as the network gained in popularity. Later, Facebook introduced Pages in 2007, giving companies and groups a way to establish a presence there and communicate with users.

Following that, Facebook Ads were introduced in 2008, giving companies a way to advertise on the platform and target particular demographics. Now, social media has become an integral part of our daily lives, serving as a platform for social interaction, content sharing, and instant online accessibility. With its dependable and immediate features, social media has created ample opportunities for businesses, especially in the realm of online marketing.

Social media marketing has enabled companies to reach their desired audience quickly and efficiently, allowing them to communicate with consumers in real-time and tailor their messages to meet their needs.

Why is Social Media Marketing Important?

In today's digital age, social media marketing has become an essential component of modern business strategy. For the church, social media can and should be considered our new mission field. With the vast majority of people active on social media platforms, businesses and non-profit organizations that do not take advantage of this marketing tool will find themselves at a disadvantage.

Compared to traditional marketing methods such as print media, television, or radio advertising, social media marketing allows businesses to reach a large and diverse audience at a lower cost. Social media platforms provide businesses with the tools to create and share content, interact with their target audience, and establish a brand identity.

The statistical report provided by Statista projected that the worldwide expenditure on social media marketing would rise to $102 billion by the year 2023. It indicates a significant increase in the usage and importance of social media as a platform for the marketing of products and services. As social media continues to evolve and expand, it is likely that the boom in social media marketing will continue.

Most Popular Social Media Platforms— The Rise of Digital Giants

According to the latest report of Sprout Social Index, Facebook, YouTube, and Instagram are considered to be the top-listed social media platforms. And there is no doubt in saying that the usage of these social media channels is ever-increasing across the world. Facebook is still the most widely used social networking platform in the world, with over 2.8 billion active users per month. Users can connect with friends and family, join groups, and discover new content every day.

YouTube is the largest video-sharing website in the world, with over 2 billion monthly active users. As the years progressed, WhatsApp emerged and became a well-known messaging program with over 2 billion people globally.

Snapchat is another social media channel that allows its users to share photos and videos that disappear after 24 hours. It is popular among younger generations who enjoy sharing more personal and casual content with their friends.

Another interesting trend is the rise of more social

media platforms that cater to specific demographics. For example, TikTok has become popular among younger generations, with 62% of its users aged 10-29, according to Oberlo.com. LinkedIn, on the other hand, is primarily used by professionals and is popular among older generations, with 38% of its users aged 30-49.

Finding Your Perfect Social Media Platform Match

Which Social Media Platform Comes on the Top?

To determine which social media platform is the best for church marketing, you should consider the following:

Analyze Your Target Audience:

Understanding your target audience is crucial in selecting the right social media platform. Look at the demographics of your congregation, including age, gender, location, and interests. This information can help you determine which social media platforms they are most active on.

Identify the Features and Benefits of Each Platform:

Each social media platform has its unique features and benefits. For instance, Facebook is more geared towards building a community and sharing events, while X, formerly named Twitter, is ideal for quick updates and communication. Instagram and TikTok are better suited for sharing visual content, while LinkedIn is more business-oriented.

Consider the content you want to Share:

The type of content you want to share also plays a crucial role in selecting the right social media platform. If you plan to share more visual content, Instagram or YouTube may be your best option. If you plan to share more long-form content, consider Facebook or LinkedIn.

Engagement Level of Each Platform:

It's also important to look at the engagement level of each platform, such as likes, shares, and comments.

Platforms with higher engagement levels may be more effective in reaching your target audience and driving engagement. With the consideration of these factors, you can determine which social media platform is the best for your church marketing efforts. It's also worth noting that you don't necessarily have to limit yourself to one platform; you can use multiple platforms to reach a broader audience and engage with your congregation in different ways.

6 Reasons Why Your Church Needs Social Media Marketing!

Social Media Marketing can help your church reach a wider audience, connect with younger generations, increase engagement, promote events, share inspiring messages, raise awareness, drive website traffic, and do so in a cost-effective way. Here is a list of 6 reasons stating that why your church needs social media marketing:

Reach a Wider Audience:

By creating a Facebook page for your church and sharing posts about your services, events, and mission, you can reach a wider audience beyond your congregation. For example, you can use Facebook's targeting features to reach people in your local community who are interested in topics related to spirituality, faith, or religion.

Connect With Younger Generations:

To connect with younger generations, your church can use platforms like Instagram and TikTok to share behind-the-scenes glimpses/snapshots of your church life, inspirational quotes, and Bible verses. For example, you can use Instagram Stories to share short videos of your worship services or to promote events.

Increase Engagement:

To increase engagement, social media is helpful for asking questions, survey feedback, and sharing user-generated content. For example, you can ask your members to share photos of their favorite Bible verses or to share their thoughts on a recent sermon.

Promote Upcoming Religious Events:

To promote events, creating Facebook Events and sharing updates, photos, and videos is a great way to reach a wider audience.

Let's say your religious organization is hosting a conference on Mastering Finances. Here's how you could promote the event on social media:

- Create a Facebook page for your organization and an event page for the conference.
- Use eye-catching visuals of the conference venue, the keynote speakers, and other special guests.
- Include all the details of the event on the event page, such as the date, time, location, and speakers.

Share Inspiring Messages:

Of course, social media provides a platform to share inspiring messages, Bible verses, and quotes that can uplift and inspire your congregation and followers.

Drive Website Traffic:

Social Media can be used to drive traffic to your church's website, where visitors can learn more about your church, they can access resources, and connect with your congregation.

Chapter 9

Putting it all Together: From Vision to Impact

Hopefully, in the book, I offered reasons why you and your church should consider church marketing. Although the term "church marketing" raises apprehension among church leaders, the true essence of church marketing lies in adding value to people's lives. Now, let's put it all together.

Let's Start with Your Strategic Plan:

The journey to church marketing starts with your strategic plan. As stated in Chapter 5, the contents of a strategic plan will be different for each church but can include a mission or purpose statement, a vision statement, objectives, core values, and lastly, methods to monitor progress and initiate corrective adjustments.

Involve Church Leadership and Members:

Engage church leadership and members in the marketing planning process. Seek their input and feedback to ensure that the strategies align with the collective vision and values of the church. This involvement should foster a sense of ownership and ensure a diverse perspective.

Access Your Church and Its Ministries:

As discussed in Chapter 4, conduct a SWOT analysis or another type of church assessment to ensure your church and its ministries are ready to receive the people you are planning to reach. For example, if you are advertising your Children's Ministry, be sure to have the people, processes, and procedures needed to fully serve your community in this manner. One mistake in this or other areas can turn off new visitors and cause them to never return. Another good assessment tool is the "ChurchPulse" Assessment by the Barna Group. The Barna Group has provided a free set of assessment tools to help evaluate various aspects of your church, from the children's ministry to the couple's ministry, from an assessment of Faith to an assessment of Finances; the Barna Group has tools that can help.

Conduct Market Research:

You can gather information about the demographics of your community by conducting surveys or analyzing census data. A church might, for instance, run a poll/survey to learn why some members aren't consistently attending services or what kinds of events they would want to see in the future. The church could research demographic data for the surrounding community to understand the needs and preferences of the local community. This could include data on age, income, education, and religious affiliation.

Don't forget to check out "Market Research for Churches: A Beginners Guide" @ http://www.dearyoungperson.com/market-research-for-churches/ for assistance with your market research. Also, check out The Barna Group @ www.Barna.com for other great resources to begin your journey of researching trends and topics that may be important to your church and help better understand those whom your church is called to reach.

Develop Personas:

Based on your research, develop detailed profiles of your target audience. Include demographic information such as age, gender, income, and education, as well as psychographic information such as values, beliefs, and behaviors. Once you are done creating the personas, the next step is to identify their common interests.

Identify Common Interests:

Identify the interests and needs of the group represented by your persona. For example, if you have a young adult persona, hosting small groups, social events, or other activities is a great way to appeal to that group. Also, consider surveying those in this group to garner their interests and create ministries to address their needs. As a side note, some of the groups you will target may never attend a Sunday morning service. I would definitely recommend meeting and ministering to these groups where they are (online, on the basketball court, at a local coffee shop, etc.), and prayerfully, over time, they may decide to attend your church. But if they never attend your church service, consider it an opportunity to serve them wherever they are.

Develop a Marketing Strategy:

Next, create a marketing strategy. A marketing strategy is a detailed plan of all your marketing efforts (remember the 5P's). The marketing strategy should reflect the essential principles and beliefs of the church as well as include the target audience, communication channels, essential messages, and intended results.

To maintain harmony with the church's ideals, the strategy should be reviewed periodically and improved. For more information on church marketing strategies, check out "The Top 20 Church Marketing Strategies for 2023" by Vanco.

Create a Visitor-Centered website:

If you don't have a website for your church, now is the time to create one. According to a survey by Lifeway

Research, 46% of people who attend church say that a church's website was important in their decision to visit the place in person. Note, I recommend that the target audience for your website should be new visitors (the unchurch or unsaved) and not necessarily those who currently attend your church.

If you want to inform existing members using your website, I suggest having a separate section of the website specifically for members. Other options for members are creating a smartphone app or using an online website like Slack.com for internal member communications.

Additionally, Story Brand is the framework that I recommend using to ensure your church website is visitor-centered. To better understand how to create a visitor-centered website using Story Brand, listen to the "Reach the Lost" Podcast entitled "Building Visitor-Centered Websites" by Mike Ruman on Youtube.com. In this video, Mike lays out what your church website should include to focus on visitors. For example, a "Plan-A-Visit" button to allow new visitors to quickly plan a visit, a 20-second "video header background" that provides visitors with a quick overview of the life of your church, and much more.

For another resource on StoryBrand website design, listen to *"StoryBrand One Liner Exercise"* by Donald Miller on Youtube.com. In this video, Donald explains the power of creating a *"focused statement"* explaining why your church exists and why people should come visit your church.

Improve Search Performance:

The following are several steps you can take to increase the likelihood that your church will be found during website searches.

Local "Search Engine Optimization (SEO)":

According to a <u>Pew Research Center</u> survey, 37% of people who attend religious services believe that proximity to their home is the most important factor when choosing a church. This means that when someone searches for phrases like "churches near me," your church has a better chance of showing up in their search results as long as you're located within the defined geographic area. Without spending a lot of money on advertising, you can bring in new members by optimizing your website and online presence for local search.

Use Relevant Keywords:

Use relevant keywords in your website's title tag, Meta description, and content. For example, if your church is located in Los Angeles, make sure to use keywords such as "Los Angeles church," "Christian church in LA," and "spiritual community in Los Angeles" in your website content.

Also include terms like "divorce," "drug addictions," "fostering," "food pantry, "or other services provided by your church or nonprofit organizations that your church can recommend or is associated with.

Establishing relevant keywords is an important step in ensuring your church is relevant in the minds and hearts of those you are trying to reach.

Create High-Quality Content:

Your website's content should be informative, engaging, and relevant to your target audience. You can also include blog posts, podcasts, and videos that address the needs and interests of your target audience. For example, Hillsong Church has a strong online presence and uses a blog and newsroom, which are updated regularly to stay engaged with those who are interested in their church.

Optimize your Website's Structure:

Make sure your website is structured for easy navigation. Use clear headings, subheadings, and bullet points to break up your content and make it more readable. Victory Church Atlanta is a great example of an easy to navigate website. They have a well-structured website with clear navigation and easy access to sermons, serving, giving, and much more.

The Use of Hashtags:

Including hashtags in your social media posts is an efficient way to increase visibility on platforms such as Twitter, Instagram, and TikTok. By using relevant hashtags, you can make your content more discoverable to those seeking information in your area of expertise or interest.

If you're sharing spiritual content such as Gospel messages or quotes, using hashtags like

➜ #God Heals
➜ #Gospel of Jesus
➜ #Church Family
➜ #God's Word

These can enhance the promotion of your uplifting message to a broader audience. Additionally, you can collect contact information from people who visit your social media profile by using META tags or Instagram quick forms. As a result, "clicks" on your church's social media website can become "connections."

Use social media and other digital platforms:

A well-crafted social media marketing plan/strategy is essential for churches looking to attract more visitors, engage the wider community, build a strong online presence, and share their message effectively.

Again, the key to success is to develop a clear understanding of your target audience, their needs, preferences, and the platforms they use most frequently. Creating relevant and engaging content that resonates with your audience fosters a sense of community, encourages engagement, and ultimately helps to drive attendance and fosters active participation.

Navigating the complex world of social media marketing for churches can be challenging, especially when you are new to marketing or unfamiliar with the latest trends and best practices. Facebook, Twitter, and Instagram are valuable tools for reaching potential visitors. Creating your church's profile on these platforms can help you to connect with more people in your local area.

Don't know how to create a Facebook ad or what to post on your Social Media channels? *Don't worry!* I recommend reviewing the 3-part series by Chris Abbott on *"What to Post on Church Social Media"* and *"How to Create a Facebook ad."* Both videos, along with a ton of other videos available on Youtube.com, can show you the way.

Add Your Church to the "Google Listing":

Google listing allows you to create a free business profile (both for profit and non-profit) about your church. Adding your church's website to this online directory is a great way to increase awareness of your church. When your church is listed with Google listings, more information about your church will be displayed during a website search, making it simpler for people to find relevant information about your church.

How to Fund Google Marketing:

The Google Ad Grants program provides eligible nonprofit organizations with up to $10,000 per month in advertising credits to be used on Google Ads. However, to qualify for Google Ad Grants, your organization must be an eligible nonprofit, have a high-quality website that meets our website policy, and be able to meet the program policies.

See https://www.google.com/grants/faq/ for more information. There are many companies positioned to help churches and other non-profit organizations qualify for the Google Ad Grant. ReachTheLost.com, ClickNonProfit.com, and MissionalMarketing.com just to name a few.

Create an App for Your Church

It's understandable that not all churches may have the financial means to invest in an app through a centralized platform.

If your church is financially able to create an app, the Church Co @ https://thechurchco.com/ is one of the many companies that can help you build your first church app. If you don't have the financial means to build your church app, visit SmartChurch.com for access to their free app. Either way, having an app for your church is a great way to foster internal church communication.

My Final Thoughts!

Within the pages of this book, hopefully, you have discovered a wealth of insights, strategies, and practical suggestions to propel your church's message and mission to new heights. Drawing inspiration from biblical principles, marketing theories, and real-life examples, this guide illuminates the path to spreading the good news with integrity and purpose. Whether you are a seasoned church leader seeking to revitalize your marketing efforts or a newcomer ready to make a profound impact, I hope this book is your indispensable companion. I hope it provides the knowledge, guidance, and inspiration you need to navigate the ever-changing landscape of church marketing, ensuring that your message resonates and reaches those who need it most.

Now, take a moment to reflect on the small steps you can take right now to embark on your church marketing journey. Remember, every stride forward is progress! You can expand your influence and convey the authenticity that distinguishes your church by understanding the needs of your target audience. Also, amplifying your church's unique message, creating a captivating online presence, and embracing interactive community engagement through social media and events. In the end, your marketing efforts should flow from your basic beliefs and mission, creating strong bonds with both current and potential church members.

To avoid feeling overwhelmed, take your time and don't attempt to complete everything at once. Start off small and progressively increase your efforts. Choose one area for growth in your church and concentrate on developing it. Don't be reluctant to seek advice and assistance from other church leaders or specialized church marketing companies. Focus on the special work God is doing inside your congregation, and don't compare your church to others.

Consider producing things that can point visitors in the direction of your church, acting as a trail of breadcrumbs that direct them to discover and interact with your church. These breadcrumbs may consist of training, community events, or highlighting special occasions that stimulate people's curiosity and motivate them to visit your church. Keep in mind that progress and growth will take time, but don't let your message go unheard. Embrace the power of effective church marketing and embark on a transformative journey from start to finish.

If you are interested in connecting with me or would like for me and my team to help with your church marketing efforts, you can reach us at info@relevancemm.com. Finally, I have provided names of companies within this book to help your church along its marketing journey. I am not providing an endorsement of any particular company but rather offering resources for your church to use.

*So now, let's embark on the mission to market your church, reach more people, and grow your church to the **Glory of God.***

Thank You Note for Readers!

"To all the church pastors, nonprofit leaders, and marketing gurus who took the time to read this book, thank you for giving my words a chance."

www.ingramcontent.com/pod-product-compliance
Lightning Source LLC
Chambersburg PA
CBHW051324120626
46547CB00015B/2381